Divine Infinite Love

Nash Ndemo

Copyright © **January 2013**

All rights reserved.

This publication may not be reproduced, in whole or in part, by any means including photocopying or any information storage or retrieval system, without the specific and prior written permission of the author and publisher.

This book is sold subject to the condition that it shall not, by way of trade or otherwise, be re-sold, hired out, or otherwise circulated without the author's or publisher's prior consent in any form of binding or cover other than that in which it is published and without a similar condition including this condition being imposed on the subsequent purchaser.

First Edition: January 2013
Published by Nsemia Inc. Publishers (www.nsemia.com); Oakville, Ontario, Canada

Edited By: Charles Phebih-Agyekum
Cover Concept Illustration: Nash Ndemo
Cover Design: Danielle Pitt
Layout Design: Kemunto Matunda

Note for Librarians:
A cataloguing record for this book is available From Library and Archives Canada.

ISBN: 978-1-926906-29-4

To all the love in my life: my whole family, friends and acquaintances, my teachers and professors, mentors and coaches, and to EVERYONE at large, to divinity at whole, and to LOVE at most, and forevermore to its infinity

TABLE OF CONTENTS

Acknowledgements --------------------------------------- vii
Foreword -- ix
About the Author --------------------------------------- xii

BEAUTY

Let us be lovers --------------------------------------- 3
Your Smile --- 4
Her Touch -- 5
Dancing Flames of Love --------------------------------- 5
Breath of Love --- 6
It Blooms -- 6
Allure --- 7
A Breeze --- 8

BLUES

Love a Little -- 11
Don't Speak of Love ------------------------------------ 11
When will Love Bloom ----------------------------------- 12
Patiently Waiting -------------------------------------- 13
What is real? -- 15
Hope --- 15
What Am I Supposed to Do ------------------------------- 16
Where There is Smoke ----------------------------------- 16
My Only Experience is You ------------------------------ 17
We Withhold Whilst We Wait ----------------------------- 17
Flight if My Love -------------------------------------- 18
Do You Care? --- 19
How Could You Leave ------------------------------------ 20
Don't Forget --- 20
Even So -- 21
Deeply Despondent -------------------------------------- 21
I am Weeping --- 22
A Drop Then Love Then? --------------------------------- 23
Will You Miss Me --------------------------------------- 24
See You Tomorrow --------------------------------------- 24

My Decision to Love You ----------------------------- 25
You Choose to Let Go -------------------------------- 25
All This Time -- 26
Never Too Late to Love ------------------------------ 26
A Night under the Sky ------------------------------- 26
The Secret to Greatness ----------------------------- 27
I'll Keep Singing I'll Keep Dreaming ---------------- 27
Bloated Ink Watery Lines Clear Love ---------------- 28
If She Only Knew ------------------------------------ 29
Tears' Weight -- 29
Forever Smiling -------------------------------------- 30

ECSTASY

1. Look --- 31
2. My View from the Sky --------------------------- 32
3. Tell me -- 34
4. Ahh -- 34
5. Mystery in my Attraction of You ---------------- 35
6. Oh My Dear ------------------------------------- 36
7. All is all I Give --------------------------------- 36
8. O So Tight -------------------------------------- 37
9. You have No Control --------------------------- 38
10. Listen --- 39
11. True Love -------------------------------------- 39
12. The Music of Silence -------------------------- 40
13. Can We Go Slowly Today? -------------------- 41
14. There is more to this -------------------------- 42
15. That Sound ------------------------------------ 43
16. The Acme Arrival ------------------------------ 44
17. Wow -- 45
18. Slow Down ------------------------------------- 46
19. I have You ------------------------------------- 46
20. Trading This ----------------------------------- 48
21. Never Say Never ------------------------------- 49
22. Dream Song ----------------------------------- 50
23. What Would You Do for Love? --------------- 51
24. A Natural Attraction --------------------------- 52
25. Tell Me When ---------------------------------- 53

INSPIRATIONAL LOVE

1. How Else to Understand Love --------------------57
2. How Will I Know ----------------------------------57
3. Maudlin ---57
4. Arise and Go --------------------------------------58
5. To Be What You Want-----------------------------58
6. Answer --58
7. Life --59
8. Feel This Freedom --------------------------------59
9. Just Dance and You Will Know This Love -------60
10. Remember to Blink and Breathe ----------------60
11. A Truth of Fear and Love -------------------------62
12. I Worship your Love -------------------------------63
13. Astral --64

LOVE

1. Love ---67
2. Phoofesheeshs -------------------------------------68
3. Take a Flight with Love ---------------------------68
4. That is Why We Kiss -------------------------------69
5. I love Those Lips ----------------------------------70
6. Her Eyes When She Wakes ------------------------72
7. Let Us Be --73
8. When Time Ceases to Exist -----------------------73
9. Bliss ---74
10. Cast a Spell of Love -----------------------------75
11. Fantasy or Reality -------------------------------75
12. Too True To Be Good ----------------------------76
13. Lo the gods long this love ------------------------76
14 A Breathing Poem of Love -------------------------77
15. Dialogue of Love ---------------------------------79
16. Listen 'Tis the Sound of Poetry -------------------81
17. I Closed My Eyes and Believed ------------------82
18. I Choose You -------------------------------------83
19. Love Like Lotus ----------------------------------84

20. Love of the Zodiac --------------------------------85
21. Magnetic Love -----------------------------------86
22. Baffled Zodiac -----------------------------------87
23. Contiguous Countenance ------------------------87
24. Tangled --88
25. Guide Me O' Divine Spirit -----------------------89
26. What if --89
27. Why Wait for Love -------------------------------90
28. Forgiveness -------------------------------------90
29. My Only Need -----------------------------------91
30. Possibility --------------------------------------91
31. Only ---92
32. My Only Request --------------------------------92
33. Rose Bush --------------------------------------93
34. What is True Love -------------------------------94
35. I Suddenly Awake and Wrote of You ------------94
36. Our Love --95
37. You and I ---------------------------------------96
38. Tears at Midnight-------------------------------97
39. Thief --98
40. Loss or Gain? -----------------------------------99
41. Awareness is Connection ----------------------101
42. Crimson Love ----------------------------------102
43. My Miracle is your Love -----------------------103
44. My Meaning of Life and Death -----------------104
45. My Last My All ---------------------------------105

ACKNOWLEDGEMENTS

I would like to especially thank Eddie Kegode, my former high school teacher, for an exceptional meritorious foreword of this book. I would like to thank all my teachers and all those who recognized my talents and encouraged me to pursue success and contribute something positive to this world. I also thank everyone and anyone who read my works before this publishing. True gratitude may be arduous to express; but my gratitude at this moment, is truly a silent stream flowing with many thanks from an endless unknown space in my heart: to bless all those important to me, who keep me inspired, full of life, and full of love. May my poetry stream bounty of peace and love to whomsoever! Thank you.

FOREWORD

When a few years ago, Nash and I exchanged Facebook banter on his virtual wall that led to a 'poem' of sorts; I was therefore not surprised when I found myself reading this anthology.

Clearly a manifesto to love, the poetry in this collection is evocative and reminiscent of Angolan poet Antonio Jacinto's *Letter from a Contact Worker* where Jacinto invokes the ministration of nature's powerful elements - the wind, the animals, the birds, the bees and the fish to take his message of love to his lover. Unfortunately for Jacinto, the persona in his poignant poem cannot write; nor his lover read. For those who can however, Nash Ndemo pens very vivid and moving poetry invoking all of nature's efficacious elements to bring his message of love alive to his audience.

The subject of Love has never been an easy one to deal with because of its inherent capricious nature. To many, love means a variety of things. Some say it is a powerful all consuming emotion- a high virtue; and yet to others it is the work of a metaphysical Cupid. It is no wonder that with so many varying viewpoints, one still cannot capture as closely as this anthology attempts to, the true meaning of love.

Nash Ndemo clearly demonstrates that love is not a sign of weakness; it is a sign of strength. Just as Luther Vandross croons in his songs about "The Power of Love", so does Ndemo parade the ability- through his pulsating poetry- to capture the beating heart marching to the throes of love. The sheer raw power of love captured in verse.

Having seen Nash's writing develop over the years, I am in no way surprised at his bold attempt to tackle, in poetic form, a subject that has hitherto been considered 'unmanly' or weak in the African context. To show open affection was- and still is – considered by some to be taboo in 'manly' Africa. It is not uncommon to hear cynics and naysayers condemning love as the work of witches, potions and the supernatural. Nash begs to differ.

To talk of love; to show affection; or even to pretend to be "in love" is a subject that many African writers have tackled; but have often come across as sympathisers of superstition and witchcraft. In Elechi Amadi's "The Concubine" for instance, three men who fall in love- nay are 'bewitched' by the betrothed of a sea god- each meet an unfortunate and terrible death. It is not uncommon in the African tradition to blame *Mami Wota*, or other deities for what comes naturally. Nash does not do this.

Aptly titled, **Divine Infinite Love**, this anthology refreshingly dips into nature and arouses all the senses. It invokes the spirituality of love inviting the reader on a well woven journey through a landscape filled with picturesque sketches that transports the reader into the gardens of love.

In recent times, Kenya has seen a sudden freshness of literary and artistic expression. New names are taking up the mantles once held by David Cook, Jonathan Kariara and Jared Angira.

That Kenya is experiencing a renaissance in poetry is without doubt, and Nash is basking in this sudden warming and new awakening of Kenyan writers and artists who have not shied away from the challenge that this rebirth has thrust upon the East African stage. With poets like Nash, and others who are bursting onto the scene, the future for African writing is bright.

Nash's love for artistic expression was noticed while he studied at the St Mary's School Nairobi where as a young scholar, he participated in Theatre Arts and the school annual Musical. I noticed Nash's work, however, in the classroom. He is a bold writer who will not follow the mundane and thoroughly trodden beaten path; he is willing to take his pen in a different direction and that in my view- quite akin to Robert Frost's poem *The Road not Taken*- is what makes the difference between exceptional and outstanding.

In his poem *Her Touch*, the musicality and mastery of expression arouses all the senses; suddenly I am transported to this place where only a gifted craftsman can take you. I hear music, I smell the aroma and I taste the air, I touch love. The mind's eye is awakened!

> *"Her hair chimes with aroma*
> *As the wind swiftly passes through every strand*
> *From a distance her beauty is like music*
> *My eyes can hear her sound of beauty as it echoes in my heart*
> *And shakes a feeling of love"*

Ndemo also tackles the subject of unrequited love, and the bitterness of separation in: *What am I Supposed to do?* and *Patiently Waiting*. At one point Nash feels that he has talked about love so much that it ceases to feel real. It is real and it is captured in his poetry.

Love is in the air; love is in the wind; love is everywhere and just as Ella Wheeler Wilcox's poem *Love's Coming* predicts, Nash's poetry has arrived like a "...prince to claim his bride...". This is a legitimate proclamation of love in its purest form. It is bold, unwavering and focused.

For those who are too cynical to believe in love this anthology will dare them to dream and challenge them to delve into the depths of their innermost feelings and senses. It will invite even the most hardest of hearts to take the plunge.

It really does not matter what language one speaks; love is a universal language and clearly this collection is penned in the language of love.

I have no doubt whatsoever that this poetry will be refreshing to those who are willing to let Nash take them with him on this journey through the heart- to hear the music and feel the pulsating beat of hearts in love.

Edwin Kegode
Head of Drama
Meadows School, Kent, UK

ABOUT THE AUTHOR

Nash Ndemo is a distinguished poet from Kenya who currently based in the USA. One of his poems *A Breathing Poem of Love* was featured in a collection of short works titled "Expressions 3". Another one titled *The Voice* was featured in "Forever Spoken", an anthology and won an editor's choice series award and was later produced into a spoken word form titled "The sound of poetry".

His inner poet was roused in Kenya after exposure to different forms of African poems and literature while attending St Mary's School in Nairobi. Here he experienced rich literary forms written or spoken in English and Kiswahili. On moving to North America, he was exposed to more literature dating far back as ancient Greece to the contemporary. He says his inner poet fully awakened at the moment he heard Sappho's poetry, "I was amazed how someone's voice could echo from ancient Greece to a cold 8:00 am English class." Later, while attending Tabb High (Virginia), he contributed a number of poems for his school's literary magazines. His poetry was warmly welcomed by a visual Arts Professor at Hampton University (Virginia) who took it as a graded project for Nash to read his poetry aloud for the students to interpret into painted depictions.

Nash manages to balance his creative work in writing and art with quite some humour that caught the attention of Jay Leno, who featured him and his colleague on the tonight show in a "Christmas Pranks" NBC special that aired live on 12/21/11. An article about this appearance was later published in his college's press, the Mace & Crown student newspaper of Old Dominion University in Norfolk, Virginia.

He is currently working closely with a personal editor to break into the world of fictional novel writing.

BEAUTY

Let us be Lovers

Let us be the sea of love
To enjoy the ocean of compassion
Let us be the waves of bliss
To enjoy the waterfall of passion
Let us be the sunset of grace
To enjoy this moment of peace
Let us be the clouds of freedom
To enjoy this picture of happiness
Let us be the constellation of wishes
To enjoy this moon at midnight
Let us be the rainbow of colors
To enjoy this moment of luck
Let us be the sands of time
To enjoy this kiss forever
Let us be the hourglass of infinity
To enjoy this unity forever

Your Smile

If you knew
I would let you know
Simplicity is my notion
Facility is my motion
I don't need the entire world
All I ask
Is for your smile
In the morning
In the noon
In the night
All I need is
Your smile
And the full moon
In your enchanted eyes
When you but touch me
In the slightest manner
My chemistry changes
My heart beats a quake
When we kiss
When we kiss
When we kiss
Your lips send me afloat
To this paradise I call love
All I think of is your smile
To know I'm special
I'm on your mind
My satisfaction is your happiness
With no words how do I know?

                                        Your smile

Her Touch

She makes me long for her beauty like a kiss on a sunset
Her eyes are stronger than a vision
They make me feel weak in timidness
Her hair chimes with aroma
As the wind swiftly passes through every strand
From a distance her beauty is like music
My eyes can hear her sound of beauty as it echoes in my heart
And shakes a feeling of love
Sometimes I am overwhelmed with thoughts
Outstretched like clouds in my mind
Then when I can't bear the feeling she gives
Or when I can't tell her in words
My love comes down on a tear like a drop of rain
She hugs me and her bosom softens my heart
Her touch travels up my veins
She is magic

Dancing Flames of Desire

Her skin was as soft as the petals of a rose
Her eyes were naked gems
Reflecting the fiery furnace behind me
This is the part I love
When she fell into the spell
Of my arms
Desire
In me
Dances
As flames of a fire
Behind me

Breath of Love

I conjured you in my dream
Now you waltzed
Into my heart
To call you beautiful
Would be cliché
But your beauty is like
That of a mountain
Once you reach its peak
The view is breathtaking
So you would have to return
My breath
Otherwise to say I can't live without you
Would be a lie
Kiss me
I can't breathe without you
Lend me your love
This be the truth

It Blooms

In autumn the breeze blows and the leaves fall but still
It blooms
In winter the cold bites and the snows fall but still
It blooms
In spring everything blossoms everything rises and even more
It blooms
In summer all is bathed in warmth all is bathed in bliss and even so
It blooms
In your smile in your eyes in your heart and even in any season forever your
Beauty it blooms

Allure

Her beauty blooms like flowers of spring
Her smile glows like the brightest of all stars
Her hair sings its gold in silent serenity
Her presence is greater than a queen's
It's just enough to grace your heart in sentience
Her eyes

Forget Me Not

I'll never forget you

I'll never forget what we have
Which is forever
I'll never forget forever

Or your two eyes
                Jewels of a foreign dynasty
Or your two lips
                A smile of a foreign fantasy
Or your hair
                Strands of silky embroidery
Or your voice
                Music of a heavenly melody

Worry not
I forget to forget

                And

I remember to remember
 I'll forget you not

A Breeze

A breeze through her hair
Like a breeze through bristles of fur
Like a breeze through soft fields of grass
Is like tracing the meandering path of a passing zephyr

The gravity of her eyes
Like the moon
Pulling me toward my dream
My dream of love and flight to it

Does love exist?
Or do I make it exist?
Or do I open awareness to its existence?
This is life or death and love between

In her presence
I am as a flag captive to the wind
Anywhere she briskly blows I billow
Anywhere she freely flows I follow

BLUES

Love a Little

If I read you my poetry
You would drown in tears
If I showed you all my love
Your heart might halt
So bit by bit I slowly satisfy you
Drop by drop you bathe in my waters
We have all the time for this greatness
The journey begins with our lips
Can you feel the ground anymore?
I have inverted this law of gravity
Now we gravitate to the moon
Let's levitate on love

Don't Speak of Love

When I first laid my eyes on her that's all I did
Her eyes were blooming daisies
Eyelashes soft slender and petals of blinking bliss
My heart was as light and as swift as a hummingbird
Quick to fall in love but gentle to levitate in joy
Overwhelmed by a nectar so sweet
Of a fountain of youth so bounteous
On a flower I call my first kiss
Her skin was like satin
So soft imagination must liken it to clouds
Only to suffice as reality
Her touch was a threat and a comfort
My solar plexus had an intermittent paroxysm and pacification
I cried and she cried and the rain cried
I had to let her know because how would she know?
What if she didn't know?

What if she knows?
I don't know
I love you I told her blasphemy I uttered
Love vanished and reappeared weakened thenceforth
The petals of my beautiful flower began to fall with the wind
And my love began to fall with chance
She loves me she loves me not
Beware don't speak of love it won't exist

When Will Love Bloom

I write about love
But you don't read it
I sing about love
But you've never heard it
I draw about love
But you've never seen it
When will you know?
How much I love you

Patiently Waiting

An apple grows in my throat
As I hold back my tears
And listen to the rain

My heart is full of love
But speaking of it
Will not make you see it

I have transformed
Into a force of potential
My wings grow

But I still patiently wait
Humble and resolute
For a journey of two

I am perched on this rock
This fortress this steadfast fortress
Gazing unto the sea and its turbulence

The world knows not
Because I have hidden myself
For your love for your touch for your kiss

> I am heaven and earth
> An angel and human
> A spirit and soul

> I am in conflict
> Because I am human
> Because I am in love

> I need not a message in a bottle
> My words touch your heart
> This instant this moment this time

> I feel you I feel what you're feeling
> I understand you I know what you know
> Can I be a helping hand?

> It is cold on this rock
> The wind has a grip of winter
> The clouds lay low with dew

> I am clothed with my wings
> Still patiently waiting
> Waiting to feel you draw near

The world is big when I am alone
The universe is immense when I am alone
Space is endless time is infiniteness

The world is small when I am in love
The universe is infinitesimal when I am in love
Space is a venture time is imagination

I was ambitious when I was alone
I was prospective when I was alone
Materials were a ravenous abyss

I am a poet when I am in love
I am a romantic when I am in love
Nothing is more important than your eyes than your smile

I glance around me still standing on this rock
I thought I heard your voice calling my name
I thought I smelt your scent your sweet flowery scent

Love is the greatest thing that happened to me
Love is the greatest thing that happens to me
Love is the only thing that moves me

I stand here patiently waiting on this rock
Please come to me please come to my abode
All I have is this poetry and bits of your love

What is real?

I have spoken of love so much to the point it seems unreal
So I will show my love so much that you can touch it
I will prove my love so much that you can kiss it
This is my gift of hope and patience
For the greater good to come
There is no future without hope
There is no past without memories
I will arrive on wings
Or on the crest of a surf
My presence will grace you
My love will melt you
So much that
It will seem unreal

Hope

I hope you don't think that every time I say I love you
I am feeding you an empty promise
My only hope is to feed you of love
Until you are full of hope
All is possible and never doubt
For only
If you are patient
For you shall see

What Am I Supposed to Do?

What am I supposed to do?
I sit here in silent passion
Communicating to you in silent poetry
What am I supposed to do?
When you say leave me alone
What am I supposed to do?
When there is nothing I can do
To break this law of magnetism
I am attracted to you
You are attracted to me
But why resist?
If it's going to persist
What am I going to do?
Yes we fight yes we argue
But after that there is insatiable passion
What am I supposed to do?

Where There is Smoke

I sit here burning with desire
Blazing with passion
For you
But you see nothing
You are as calm as the emperor Nero
Silently steady as Rome burns to ash
Why not tame this flame while it is still growing?
Quench me with your lips
I need another night with you
Just me and you
And the moon glowing on our skin

My Only Experience is You

I am in everything you experience
You are in everything I experience
How then can we stop loving?
Life is an experience
My only experience is your love
My only life is you
Shall we both perish to stop this experience?
What if we fail and our love is forever?
Even so I wouldn't regret
The past troubles I would just forget

We Withhold Whilst We Wait

I'll always wait for you
If you have a heart
You would talk to me
I'll always be there
To help you through the good days and bad
I am your wish
Anything you say I will do
But I cannot force you to do anything
I cannot force you to wish
I cannot force you to believe
I cannot force you to hope
You are free to choose
My only prayer is
That you have seen what is deep inside of me
Truth honesty trust
There is only one you there is only one me
One moon one sun
One life to live
And only one love
For you and me

There is only one person who forgives
One person who waits
This person is me

Flight is My Love

I have waited for you diligently
But my wings need a little stretch
This is a test
Shall we solidify?
And look over our indifference?
I'm too excited
I'm trying to share this with you
But you show me exhaustion
Enough you say
I'm still glad my love is with you
Now we stand distant
Our barrier is but a pillow
This is that feel good stretch
After sitting for long
I choose to overlook this tiny mishap
I choose to look at the moon
Don't worry
This is a test
I'm only flying around the rock
Patience is my peace
Gravity is your promise
Flight is my love
Although
You should know
My intention mysterious one

Do You Care?

Do I have to tell you I'm dying?
For you to care
Do I have to tell you I'm lying?
For you to believe my truth
I am dead
Without your love
I am all honesty and all truth
But do you care?

I Told You

I told you the ground will shake
You didn't believe
I told you the mountain will move
You didn't believe
I told you the sea will part
You didn't believe
I told you my love
Now you believe?
Now you know I am real?

How Could You Leave?

You couldn't wait for our wishes?
Was it too hard to hope?
Was it too complicated to cope?
Why part so soon?
Was love capricious?
Are we mixed between logos and pathos?
Why couldn't you at least leave me a reason?
Why is love a mystery at first and last sight?

Don't Forget

You will have to crush your head
You will have to stab your heart
To forget me
To forget my love
For as long as you breathe
I am forever as the sun
I shall wander as wind on earth
Until it is time to part
You shall wander as waves of the sea
Until it is time to choose my heart
Trust in me
Hold my hand
I promise not to burn your soul
Of my love
Even so it will make you stronger
To love me longer
To kiss me longer
To feel me longer
Have faith in me
I will make you my goddess
Time will be a myth
Gravity a fantasy
And we'll be an exception
A favour for fervour and affection

Even So

I would have to gouge my eyes out to forget you
Even so my only memory would be
Your eyes your face your beautiful smile

I would have to blow my eardrums out to forget your voice
Even so my only music would be
Your words your laugh your melodic voice

I would have to burn my nostrils to forget your scent
Even so my only smell would be
Your skin your air your flowery hair

I would have to stab my heart to forget your love
Even so my only life would be
Your kiss your tears for me your love for me

Deeply Despondent

I'm drowning in my tears
Can you hear my gasps for breath?
I need you next to me
I need to feel your heart beat
I miss your charming voice
And the way
You make things appear bright and sunny
I can tell it and say it many times
I love you
Be free now my darling

I Am Weeping

Even gods weep
Love has no favorites
I weep for you
At midnight
Staring at the stars
Staring at the sky
Wondering at my wish
But never doubting my dreams
But ever fortifying my faith
And forever treasuring my trust
Why do we play games now?
Am I hanging bait?
You didn't give up on me
Is it because you can still mind play me?
Are all the problems
Because of my self confidence?
I cannot speak of my confidence
It is my strength
I am wise not to speak of my strengths
Lest the Philistines subdue me
And the rest of my scalp be bald
And the rest of my body linger limply
I bid you no haste but make the choice
Make the choice of love
Come with me and see the all seeing
Choose love
Choose it unconditional
Choose me
For I have chosen you
Choose not
And live an illusion for eternity
Love cannot be created
It already exists

Awaken awareness to it
And love will awaken within you
I have awakened awareness in desire
For you
Likewise will happen
Peace be with you
You should know who I am
Love be with you
I am

A Drop Then Love Then?

There is a drop of rain on my rose
Glistening sparkling
There is a drop of pain on my nose
Streaming falling
There is a drop of love in my heart
Beating teardrop
There is a drop of water in Life
Light let there be love

Will You Miss Me?

If you cannot understand my love
You will search the world
And settle with stones
Like pyrite
And one day you will realize
That you missed out
On this diamond
Hidden in a rock of innocence
On this opal
Hidden in the cavern of hope
On this emerald
Hidden in the cave of love

See You Tomorrow

I don't care about what
The stars or moon may say
My love for you is still strong
Stronger than a mountain to move
Stronger than a hurricane to blow
Stronger than any force out there

I don't care what people say
Or what people may do
They don't affect my happiness for you
My happiness with you
My happiness for us two
My happiness that I still love you

Life goes on
I'm feeling good
That's why I'm singing our song forever more
I know I'll always see you tomorrow
See you tomorrow
See you tomorrow

My Decision to Love You

I have reached the end
I have cried my last tear
I must speak and show forth
This love inside of me

I cannot control fate
I cannot control the planets
But I believe I can control decision
My decision to love you

It is time to start happening
I'm a hopeless romantic
A devout lover
An intoxicating kisser
All that you have yet to know

You Chose to Let Go

I shall continue living in my reality
You chose to forget this dream
You let go of this wish

I shall continue flying on this carpet
You chose to dismount this magic
You let go of this night

I shall continue manifesting
You chose to stop hoping
You let go of this love

All This Time

I just discovered self love
I am not heart broken
My heart has spoken
To listen is to obey
But you have done neither

Never Too Late To Love

I'm still waiting for that date
You and I will finally accept our fate
We can start a new slate
Love is never too late

A Night under the Sky

I've gone with the wind
I've taken a flight in the night
Into the moonlight
I've gone with the wind
Fare thee well so long
Sing this song bon voyage
I've gone with the wind

A Secret to Greatness

Love is secret even between lovers
Love is the invisible yet visible
Love is blind to those who cannot see it
Love is the beauty that kisses your heart
In the first few seconds of the morning
As the sun's rays grace the sea
To billow in majestic motions of wandering wind
That brushes your face with cotton bristles
And in that moment when time stops
You feel that touch that kiss
You feel waves that melt your composure into the sand
That reflects the eye of the moon in the sky
Watching two lovers so romantic that even
Cupid and all the gods of nature and all the cosmos watch
and yearn
To feel what these great two are feeling as one
That was me a long time ago
Now I am one piece missing another
Patiently waiting for my other
Piece of love to become great again

I'll Keep Singing I'll Keep Dreaming

I just want you to know
That I love you
So I'll keep on singing
I'll keep on dreaming
Of the day you'll open your heart
To our love
So let go of the past
You'll never relive it
Can you believe it?
Let go of all the hurt pain tears

You have all my trust
That it won't happen
So please open up your heart
To my love
So please open up your mind
To my kind words
Everyday
Is why I'll keep singing
Is why I'll keep dreaming
Of the day we'll say forever
I do
And never
Adieu

Blotted Ink Watery Lines Clear Love

I wrote about you and I cried
Why does this distance exist between us?
I am here you are there
But in love together we are here

You thought about me and you cried
Why does this kiss last forever?
I closed my eyes you closed your eyes
Integrity we share trust we bear

I remember the first I love you and I cried
Why haven't I been loved in a long time?
My heart is yours your heart is mine
Together we love forever in time

He wrote about you and he cried
He hoped and he believed but the pain had to be relieved
I had to finish this last verse for him who cried
O the tears that wet this page O the ink that wrote this
love woe he died

If She Only Knew

Sometimes
Love is just a knowing
Maybe she'd cry
If she knew
I loved her so much
I woke up
Every morning
Reciting poems
Of our love
Reciting her name
Like the birds
Reciting bliss
Of a morn' Sun
If she knew
If she only knew
She'd surely cry

Tears' Weight

Your pink lips turned to purple
Silent tremors of an internal storm
Of sentiment and sadness
Brewing from the core
I watched as it rose up
To your cheeks
Red
Nose jittering
And finally
To your eyes
Like the weight of heavy rain clouds
The dew did drop
You tried to hide this pain from me
But I only felt it stronger

I still feel your cold teardrop
On my finger
Many years after softly
Wiping the smooth valley
Of your cheek
Be happy my love
Be free

Forever Smiling

That smile that smile
When I see that smile
Radiating at me from across a mile
Or across the ocean
Or across time
Like the setting sun
Or like the rising moon
I know it is love
Because you are the one
The one that I'd like to swoon
I am not burning
I am radiating too
I am smiling and smiling just for you
When our eyes merge as two oceans
As a blend of colours dark and bright
And when our lips embrace in meandering motions
The velvet behind our eyes sends us soaring beyond the skies
It feels good to kiss and smile
It feels good to kiss and smile
Now I see my smile forever in your smile
Now I feel your smile forever in my only lonely smile

ECSTASY

Look

Come and see the landscape from my point of view
Come and feel all the love that I have for you

Breathe this air so full of flowers' perfume
Touch every petal your magic makes them bloom

Dance and be happy every moment is a gift
Sing your heart out my soul you uplift

My View from the Sky

If mountains were clouds
We could fly over a rainbow
And mount on a magical pedestal
And watch the storms move by
The ground wouldn't shake
Of a rumbling thunder
Or an earthquake asunder
We are suspended in the air
Gravity is a choice
To move here or to move there
Swirl with me
Through the ice cream clouds darling
I'll twirl you
And furl your hair like soft cotton candy
I'll kiss your lips with such fragility
You will be drunken of ecstasy
And you will experience
A glimpse of being a god in the heavens
All the abundance of this earth
Is ours to share and blessing to bear
Cry with me in gratitude and grace
Lo look at the sunset

Our tears have morphed to diamond crystals
We are all connected
The very same energy
Is in you and me
Touch me now let us be together
Kiss me now let us be forever
I love you

Tell Me

How many times should I say I love you?
As many times as my heart beats
And as many times as my lungs breathe
How loud should I say I love you?
As loud as any opera voice
And as silent as a whisper into your ear
How long should I gaze into your eyes?
Long enough that tears fall out like rain
Long enough that to blink would be insane

Ahh

It's mysterious how your thoughts manifest in to my life in to my music
    I love the mystery if it is like wine
        I'll drink it every day of my life
            My cup is my heart so fill it with your essence
                Until I get intoxicated
                just from looking in to your electric eyes
                    Light up my nights with your moon
                      And I will light up your

days with my
sun
    Let us unite
and cause an
eclipse to this
world
No one knows our secret power
Can you handle my love?
Can I handle your passion?
I am brave to say now
I love you I love your passion

Mystery is My Attraction to You

We will explore the darkness
And journey feeling fantasy in reality
Mystery is my attraction to you
You always surprise me
There is no quest
The treasure is here
My map is your body
Where do you want to go?
How do you want to feel?
Where do you want to feel it?
We'll start with my touch
Sensibility in silent flames
Blazing passion in warm heat
It is too bad darkness has to sleep
And light has to awaken
But we never sleep
We stay awaken
Caressing the night
Kissing the moon
Mystery is my attraction to you

Oh My Oh Dear

You are all the adjectives of beauty
Your countenance can stop my heart
Your love can bring it back to beating
Your kiss can bring me back to life
Your words can bring me back to reality
I am wavering in your toxic attraction
I love this frenzy

All is all I Give

I will give you all the passion of my life
Passion that has tarried for this one moment
To be in your presence
To be in your light

I will give you all the love of my heart
Love that has waited for this time
To be in your spirit
To be in your world

I will give you all the desire in my body
Desire that has longed for this night
To be infused with your body and mind
To be united beyond space and time

O So Tight

A tight space
Is all a lover needs
The universe is too large

A tight embrace
Is all a lover needs
The world is too big

A small place
Is all a lover needs
This lea is too long

There is too much space
Between our lips
There is too much space
Between our hips
I need to squeeze you
Tight

Not too tight on the kiss
We might miss
The flight to the moon
And find ourselves
In a tight space

You Have No Control

When I am all over you
Sending my passion
Spreading my love
All over your skin
from paradise
Brushing your hair as soft as a bottle brush tree

You have no control
When my lips are tracing
Cupid's mark on your neck
And in your heart
There is no preparation for me
I belong not to time
Or to this force we call gravity

You have no control
Over my suggestion
Mesmerizing words of a real fantasy
I'm touching you without touching you
I make you imagine me
Even though I am before you
I'm kissing you without kissing you
I make you fantasize about me
Even though you behold me

Listen

She breathed the song of the eagle

And

She exhaled the breeze of the sea

True Love

True love is as calm as a night's breeze
That hovers across the soft waves
That reflects the billowing clouds
Of a veiled sky

True love is the blue light of the moon
That covers every surface of the night
That softens every feeling at midnight
When all is quiet

True love is slow to time
That slows the speed
That slows the movement
Of the bodies

True love chooses to last long
When it wants
When it needs and when it just desires
That true love in the making

The Music of Silence

A lover is as a thief in the night
Why he begins at the window?
I don't know
He graces his beloved
With his presence

She was only half asleep
He softly set onto her bed
As a crane sets on dark waters of a lake
Barely agitatedly
Causing but one ripple

It's a dark night
But there's just enough light
To see each other's spirit
To see her eyes
Her nose
Her smile
All looking down upon me
As the moon looks down upon a calm lake

She kisses me so happily
So glad that I made her dream a reality
We lay back and listen to the music of silence
The hypnotic monotone of one solitary cricket
Our whispers are like drops of water in a cavern
Echoing epics of love
And how it finds us and melts worries away
Cleansing our tears of troubles
Into pure diamonds of joy
There is happiness
There is freedom
In the truth of love

Can We Go Slowly Today?

I want to connect with your spirit
Through your magnetic eyes
Why are your lips softer today?
Turn the lights down low
Music?
Or would you like to listen to our touching
Brushing breathing and smooching?
These shadows make your curves
Hedonistic
I am a pilgrim of pleasure at your hallowed place
Your bosom is ballistic
The candle light has turned me into a mystic
Of your anatomy
Your slow movement today has turned me into an artist
Of your body
I babble of breasts
The slow rush for nakedness the sudden flushed feeling of
exposure
I have seen your essence unveiled
This perfect creature I crave
I am now connecting with your spirit today
You are in a trance of ecstasy
Trying to tame the crawling feet of ne plus ultra
Acquiesced ravishment
You feel flushed of fair air
A humming bird at hiatus
Its wings feathery flapping the Yoni
Spreading gracefulness and spiritual light
Around yours and my body tonight
Many thanks for going slow today

There is more to this

Science says this is the end
But I say this is the beginning
My energy is renewed
My stamina is resilient
The first few times will be earthly
The next will be spiritually
Ecstasy
You yelp for help
When there is security in my hold
You have nothing more to give
But to give in
Pour out your essence
I shall pour out my love
I understand
There is nothing left
But now to close our eyes
And continue this greatness
In another space in another time in another world

That Sound

That sound
That beautiful sound
The sound of love
And everything between love
Surrounded by love
And only limitless love

That sound
That beautiful sound
The sound in my ear
So soft so near
So warm so dear
My only dear

That sound
That beautiful sound
The sound of silence
And the fire of breathing
So hot so seething
My only feeling

That sound
That beautiful sound
The sound of love
The dance of creation
Two souls in elation
The sky my only destination

With that sound
That beautiful sound
The sound of all sound
And everything between the sound
Surrounded by the sound
And only this sacred sound

The Acme Arrival

I'm still searching my shirt for your scent
I'm still searching my mind for your memory
I'm still searching my heart for your seed of love
I'll never forget your stare
I'll never forget your subtle kiss
I still feel your small subtle lips
Tugging my lower lip
Pulling my upper lip
Your tender tongue
Tickling tasting touching
My passionate movement
Your head falling back in ecstasy
And I rushing in
Softly biting it kindly kissing it
Until you jerk back and say
Stop you are too much
My tummy is slicing itself of euphoria
You touch me tender
I touch your slender curves
Smooth skin soft thighs
Ballistic breasts
My fingers bare all the passion in one moment
One touch
You'll never forget
Even though I part
We are forever at heart
Still feeling each other
Still kissing each other
Still caressing each other
I am all gratitude
You are the one
I was waiting for
Since time

To fulfill my dreams
And my visions you drew to reality
One night in your world
Is a lifetime
Of
Sensuality and sexuality
Reality seduction subdual control
One day in my world is eternity of
Love devotion
Emotion passion and facility of fervency

Wow

'Tis all beautiful
'Tis a tear dropping from my eye
Epiphany of ecstasy
Acme of euphoria
'Tis all wonderful
'Tis my heart beating of joy
My eyes vibrant of the clouds
My eyes vivacious of the bursting splendid sun

You
Close to
Me

Slow Down

Slow this love down

Or I shall burst into ecstasy

How are we united so perfectly?

I am patience you are hope

Slow this kiss down

Or I shall murmur of love

How is my heart beating so fervently?

I am lover you are beloved

I Have You

I see the sun rise every day
 Tomorrow never dies

        I see
      The moon glow
       In your eyes
       Your beauty
        Is forever

If the sun never rises
 And tomorrow never comes
      I know forever I will see your eyes

If the Sun Stopped Shining

If the sun stopped shining
I'd have your shimmering smile
If the stars stopped shimmering
I'd have your glittering eyes
If the moon stopped gleaming
I'd have your sparkling skin

If you should ever cry
You'd still look beautiful
Your smile would radiate a rainbow

If I should ever worry
I'd still be lucky
I have your starry eyes to wish on forever

If my nights should ever fall dark
I'd still be safe
I have your light to lead me and bosom to lull on whenever

If my lungs stopped breathing
I'd have your lively lips
To clemently kiss
For one last moment to eternity
N' ifsoever heaven does not exist

I'd satiate my soul with your three words to infinity

Trading This

I was trading this feeling for love
To the sky
I wanted this kiss to last us
One hundred years

I was trading the diamonds in the sky
For your eyes
I wanted this smile to last me
One million light years

I was trading my heart
I was trading my heart
Till a tear dropped from my eye
I was trading my heart
I was trading my heart
Till the rain fell from the sky

All I wanted was one flight to the moon
So I could see this apple
In your eye
So shy to open
A crescent in the sky
A timid token
A sunset breeze
Night has fallen
This moment forever
To blink we will never
The future is wonder
The past is broken
The curse has crumbled
Love has spoken

Never Say Never

Never never say never
To love again
Don't you know love's forever
It's in you today

Come on n' take n' endeavor
To wherever amen
Wishes come true just never
Even ever ask when

Never never say never
To love again
Don't you know love's forever
It's in you today

It's an ice cream sky wherever
There's a birthday everyday
Say I love you to whomsoever
N' share this love today

Never never say never
To love again
Don't you know love's forever
It's in you today

To Love someone's not easy so together
Forgive n' pray
Always say Yea love and never
To love say Nay

Never never say never
To love again
Don't you know love's forever
It's in you today

You were born to fly
Stretch your wings and fly
Why don't you just fly?
Fly fly and fly

Dream Song

They once were all old
Where the skies would unfold
And time went by like Pharaoh
And the mountains flew by
And the ocean would cry
Its sorrowful song

But we'll never get old
And the skies would be told
That time would die an arrow
And the mountains move by
And the ocean would sigh
Its wonderful song

What Would You Do for Love

We had the whole entire swift summer for summer love
But all I have is a last minute for me to love
And you to love and we can love and be in love
What would you do for love?

I feel your tender lips taking sweet sips of breath and pain
As we kiss enjoying bliss until death we'll meet again
Will you miss me? Will you remember me? And will you
please never forget me
What would you do for love?

There's nothing to do but love
This is what I would do for love
I love you and I hope you love me too so we can be two
Together in love

Every time I look in the mirror I see your eyes
I have to fight back this feeling for me to cry
But I see your eyes I hear your cries love lift me up into
the skies
What would you do for love?

I see heaven way beyond the clouds shimmering bright as
I take a flight
I see your face in this place Venus in space love at first
sight
You're my light you're my might in the night you're my
light in spite
What would you do for love?

There's nothing to do but love
This is what I would do for love
I love you and I hope you love me too so we can be two
Together in love

A Natural Attraction

My body's a natural reaction
I swear
Your style's a wonderful distraction
I stare
Your hips your lips your eyes
Your hair
I can't move I can't breathe I can't speak
You're here
This love's causing me destruction
I can't bear
Can't you see what you're doing to me?
Do you care?

This passion's driving me to the edge
I dread
I'm hanging on the ledge by a piece of thread
I fret
Your eyes blink a seaside sunset
I shake
My heart beats a thunderous earthquake
I transpire
You touched me set my soul on fire
Apocalypse
You kissed me touched my heart with luscious lips
Satisfaction

Tell Me When?

When was the last time?
You sang with the birds

When was the last time?
You whistled with the wind

When was the last time?
You danced with the moon at night

When was the last time?
You smiled with the sun light

When was the last time?
You cried with rain drops

When was the last time?
You waved with the palm trees

When was the last time?
You waltzed with the waves of the seas

When was the last time?
You wished with a rainbow in the sky

When was the last time?
You never gave up like tomorrow

When was the last time?
You loved like there's no tomorrow

When was the last time?
You never stopped time

When was the last time?
You believed in love again

When was the last time?
You had Faith

And
You trusted in I love you forever

INSPIRATIONAL LOVE

How Else to Understand Love?

To understand poetry you must become a poet
To become a poet you must understand love
To understand love you must write poetry

To become a lover is to become a poet
To become a poet is to become a lover
Write about the lover you've become

Write about the one you love
Write about love write about nothing but love
And you will understand love

How Will I Know?

How will I know it is true love?
When you have used all of your ability
To get rid of it but the love keeps returning
Like a pole in a magnet

Maudlin?

If you're still crying
Cry your last tears
And scream
Scream your dream
Into existence
If you are still worrying
Worry no more
Love will find you
At a time
You forget time

Arise and Go

Go to the mountains hear their history
Go to the trees listen to their story
Go to the oceans harken their glory

Everything is love end of story

You Be What You Want

Be a light if you want to be a light
Be in love if you want to fall in love
Be what you want to be
Be what you really want

Answer

Tend to people's need
You might just answer a prayer indeed
For we are just an image
Not a mirage wafting in a vast desert
We are all divine energy
The eye is just shallow
The soul hallowed
Crying to merge with drops
Of the ocean deep
Yearning to love
Without debt
Unconditional love
Like the sunset

Life

If it snowed diamonds and rained gold
If leaves were emeralds and the sky a sapphire
If roses were rubies and pollen pearls
If the stars were opals and the clouds citrines
Then life itself would be valuable
And love itself would be precious
And peace alone would be a treasure
That everyone's heart could bare forever

Feel This Freedom

The sun is warm
It melts your troubles away
The ocean is clear
Your spirit is renewed
That breeze is fresh
It massages your skin
Tingling sensations of bliss and satisfaction
You have nothing to worry about
Love is everywhere

Just Dance and You'll Know This Love

Dance to the music of life
Inspire the gods
Become infinite

Dance to the music of life
Greatness is on its way
Rejoice to receive

Dance to the music of life
This song is for you
Sing and be glad

Dance to the music of life
Don't ask why life happened a certain way
Ask yourself why you are not dancing

Dance to the music of life
The future is unknown
Gamble for good play in darkness with faith

Dance to the music of life
Lightening strobes the sky
Remember you are never alone

Remember to Blink and Breathe

When the sun sets I am reminded of gratitude
When the sun rises I am reminded of grace
In every time the moon is full I think of romance I think of desire
Desire to love and share the night's nature in quiet calmness

When the rain clouds cover the sky and lay low
I feel inspired I feel overjoyed
As if something big is coming my way
Something unexpected like a surprise on a birthday

When the thunder cracks my fears are forgotten
Reminding me that there is something or someone
Great and high very high up in a firmament or heaven
Celestial or cosmic listening watching and guiding
answering and speaking to me

When I blink when I breathe
When I blink when I breathe
When I blink when I breathe

I remember there is love

A Truth of Fear and Love

Silence your fears
Listen to the thunder
Wipe all your tears
Look into the rain

Fears can be illusions
Illusions can be lies
Our fears can be a lie
Dreams can be visions
Visions can be truths
Our dreams can be true

Fire is fire and water is water
Love is fire and fear is water
Do not be afraid of love
Because fear
Love it never made
Do not be afraid of fear
Because love is never afraid
Love is the fire that burns within
Fear is the water that puts out the love
That could have been

I Worship your Love

I sit here worshiping your love
Grateful of this miracle of truth

I had no reasons
But the obstacles are the past

I had no sense
But forgiveness has worked everything out

I sit here worshiping our love
Lifting my heart a feeling so big

I just talked to you
Your words rush like adrenaline through my body

I surrendered my will
To the greatness of God

I am with patience
Forever waiting for our unification

I thought all was lost
But all is gained through faith

I am humble
I lay now on soft grass
I am content
I lay now on clouds

I am alive
I now see the realm of greatness

Astral

Waltzing with my shadow
Dreaming of Neptune
Aligning with Jupiter
For me to await my fortune
And my success and my luck

Kissing myself
Thinking of Venus
Aligning with the moon
For me to await my love
And my heart and my dearest love

Smelling water lilies
Thinking of sensuality
Aligning with sensitivity
For me to await my union
And my connection and my spirit

Looking through an emerald
Believing in green power
Aligning with protection
For me to await my clarity
And my freedom and my star

LOVE

Love

A lover has no power
He is under the curse of your love
He misses every strand of your hair
And longs to stroke each piece
He has no power
He craves the soft embrace of your lips
And the lightness of your floating fingertips
He has no power
A lover gazed upon his beloved and asked her
Am I the only one you love?
The beloved replied in the world of your love
All else has disappeared I am only present
For your stare your touch and the sensation you endlessly spread in me
In my dream time of love I have searched every space in this world
And always I return to you
Love me and I'll love you too I love you I know you love me too
Come into my abode
Let us connect on all levels of being
Together we shall befriend stars planets and gods
Hold my hand and let my love escort us into this magical realm
You have been locked in a little room of my affection
Come into my palace of love that stretches as far as the sky embraces the sea
It takes one word to describe your voice
And a thousand to describe your beauty
But all the philosophers sages and great thinkers have endlessly contemplated
On one question what is the true color of love? But in one blink and one thought I say
It is in your eyes

Phoofesheeshs

The stars sparkle in her eyes
The moon glows on her face

The breeze plays with her hair
Her smile makes my heart sizzle

Her kiss makes my lips tickle
Her fingers swirl with my chi

Her fingertips twirl with my chakras
Her hands awaken butterflies

The smell of sensation sea salty air
The music of the night

Shwoosh waves crashing
Phoofesheeshs palms rustling

Take a Flight with Love

We sat on a cloud and kissed until the sun set to embrace
the sea
I stroked her hair like a Spanish guitar
And touched her body with musical notes
And the sounds she made were like a sensual saxophone
My hand softly slid down her side and sculpted into her
hips of
Contours as rich as a viola's
My other hand softly traveled down her back
A harmonic curve as smooth as a golden harp
We had all the little grains of sand to count in the
hourglass except
Time doesn't really exist when there is no gravity

I stared into her round dark eyes and saw the reflection of love
I kissed her again and again to make music of our lips
Drops of mysterious echoes
We flew down into the night
Everything was quiet just the whistling wind in our ears
I held her hand tightly as we slowed down to look over a lake
Two shadows ruffling ripples
And making the blue moon dance in the magic of midnight
We settled upon a golden grassy field to watch Zephyrus move here and there
We made zodiacs of the stars and made a thousand wishes with the meteor showers
We took a flight with love

That's Why We Kiss

We kiss because there is no expression left
After our impression of nature at night
And the sound of a solitary bird
Whistling in the wind of rain to come
We kiss because there are no more words to say
I love you is not enough
So we kiss and our touch sends sensations
Up and down the spine
To spark the sleeping butterflies in our bellies
To flap their wings of a feathery feeling
We kiss because our lips combine into an elixir
Leaving us with a drunken daze
For each other's eyes
We kiss because we are renewed of energy
Indescribable I just babble
Like I fell from the tower of Babel
Incoherent as to what my body is feeling
Supernaturally so I just

Babble making bubbles
Tasting tears and then we kiss again and again
Switching sides up and down
Speeding up giving and taking
Taking a break to breathe in and out
In through the nose
And out through the lips
Still touching together and then
Relaxation and a sigh of satisfaction settle us
And bewilders both of us
Who are trying to touch something intangible
Something as someone's soul but it feels great
And gratifying to keep trying and trying
Kissing and kissing
And that's why we kiss

I Love Those Lips

I fall asleep
With a subtle smile
This feeling
Like standing close to the edge
Of a tremendously tall building
Perceiving depth creates
This hysteria
One cannot fully perceive love
It is just a simple
Magical understanding
It is there without question
I never question your pink lips
Your beauty melts this snow
The blush on your cheeks is proof
There are too many ways
Lovers conjure to express love
I prefer this nonexistent language
Knowing there is nothing to prove

With our love
I prefer this stare
When I move out of my body
To dance with your spirit
And to waltz atop the clouds of your dreams
I prefer giving up
On trying to document
The phenomena of our presence
I love that thing
Your pink lips do when you sleep
I love the way
I love how
I simply love
Zzzzzz

Her Eyes When She Wakes

I woke up in the morning
And gazed at my love
And realized that sleeping is not an ordinary action
It is an act of beauty that God so graced
Her breathing was so slow and sensual
I watched her dream
Because dreaming is infinite
It is the abode of the great consciousness
Wherewithal we wonder in endless possibilities
I can still feel my fingers touching her skin
Arousing butterflies to spread nectar so sweet
Around her lavender skin
Her ribcage expanded in ecstasy
She breathed deeper upon feeling
My soft kiss and tender tongue
I learned about three things that moment
How love can surmount any barriers
How my gaze will never change
And how important ballet is
After arising from bed
With the gravity of a cloud
Even though
She sensed me leave her warmth and woke up
When I looked into her eyes
I discovered there is no stone more precious than this pair

Let Us Be

Let us watch the first rays of the sunrise
Let us breathe in a new day of love
And annex a few drops of tears to the sea
Let us add the sounds of our kisses
To the whooshing waves
And our soft sighs to the whispering wind
May our feelings echo across frequencies and fields
And our love beyond phenomenon and philters

When Time Ceases to Exist

When my feet sink into the warm sands
And my ears tune into the sound of waves
And my eyes stare upon an endless sky
And I take a breath of a beautiful breeze
I find that time ceases to exist

When my hand unites with hers
And where all else is blinded except our stare
And our lips are caught in a passionate embrace
And our love burns ever more for each other
I find that time ceases to exist

Bliss

I was calm I was warm
I was content on that lazy afternoon
I looked out the open window
To watch a briskly breeze bring a little speck of cotton
To settle on my love's eyelashes
Her eyes were a glimpse of the bluest sky
I was set free by every blink
Like a white seagull that casts a shadow over white sands
Who's coy is carried by a sea's breeze
Or like a beautiful blackbird free to roam forests dark and deep
Wide and wild
Or like a singing nightingale
Free to sing a lullaby
Free to sing a symphony
Free to sing a song

I was happy

Cast a Spell of Love

Come with me into this world of mystery
Where the sun glows red
And where the moon glows blue
Walk with me in this velvety darkness
Where our skin glows shades of spiritual light
Breathe with me this soft air of ecstasy
Where our souls ignite passion for each other
And our hearts unite and we become infinite
Stare with me into the endless sky
Where the purple sea seems to join
The floating burgundy clouds
There is no time in this place
It is a journey of magik
Where powers of the unknown
Cast spells of good
That abracadabra
Can be real

Fantasy or Reality

Love seems a fantasy
When there is great distance between lovers
Love seems a fantasy
When there is great contiguity between two lovers
Love is real yet magical
Just don't look for explanations
As to why we levitate on this kiss
Just don't look for a reason
As to why my touch is telekinetic
Just don't look for logic
As to why my thought is psychic
You will search in vain

Too True To Be Good

Let's shower in the stars
And glitter like gold
Let's drink milk of the crescent moon
And recline like newborns
Let's inhale the clouds
And blow smoke rings of hearts and love
Let's kiss and cry
And make a rainbow from teardrops
Let's glide and sing like the birds
And whistle and hum melodies
Of lullabies like the birds
Let's love like true love
Like true unconditional love

Lo the gods long This Love

The simplicity of you and me
Our imagination
Soaring beyond earth and space
Stopping between
To dally upon a blanket of clouds
As red as the setting sun
But your pink lips
Adding a hue
To this magnificence
In silence
Just the music
Of our lips
Sounds of kisses
Echoing in silence
Drops
Of mysterious
Lakes
Hidden in taverns

Of wide and deep
Of dark and magic
O the gods envy our embrace
We are a masterpiece in nature
Painted by the setting sun
And now
The wind
To carry us
Far and away
With love

A Breathing Poem of Love

I tell you of things I've seen and felt
When I stood upon the beach and watched
As every detail of nature moved in beauty
And how my heart did beat

I saw the sun set in her blithesome red orange
And watched as all the shadows united to become night
I listened to the palm trees mimicking the waves of the sea
And felt the tender breeze touch upon my skin

I looked up into the sky
Where the stars gallantly glittered
Sparkled and twinkled around a bright fluorescent milky moon
To my heart the beauty of night I did really feel

I used to be alone in this garden
Until my father blessed me with one like myself
Now it is love that is an obsession
Thinking on't I can never stop

When my eyes become as night
I have dreams of the precious one I love
As if I long to have her by my side
And long to feel her in my heart

Then she comes to lie next to me
Like that tender breeze upon my skin
Her movement in nature so light
Her presence gracefully blesses like that of Eve

I marveled about the beauty of night
But she is more than this beauty
Her bosom is the softest of feathers
That when I lay upon them I fly to the round milky moon

Thence my heart feels
Hence my heart beats
No longer for ticking time
But thusly beats with everlasting love

Her lips are the red orange
Like the setting sun
That I passionately kiss
Always in everlasting bliss

Her nose is the conductor of her breathtaking beauty
She breathes sensation just like a flute
My passion crescendos
And my body sparkles as my heart sings for love

She drifts me to ecstasy
Her love could melt snow
She swells me with pleasure
To my ears sweet is her tender touching voice

Her eyes blind me in glamour by every blink
We stare at each other in mesmerizing romance for one another
Her hair is a golden cascading waterfall
Gracefully combed by a breezy wind

Her footsteps press lightly as piano keys
And flamboyantly sound like the 'Moonlight Sonata'
O the way she moves the way she moves
She walks with beauty on top of drops of rain

A Dialogue of Love

Tears like rain can be of happiness or pain
I cry thy beauty in a thousand wishful words

Enjoying this silence and the sound of nothing
My sleep is hardest to fight when you are next to me
Your love for me is a
beautiful curse
Under its spell I am powerless
So the sky is my home
I am ever changing like the clouds
I float and wonder what it is like to love you
In a different language

Tears like rain can be of happiness or pain
I cry thy beauty in a thousand wishful words

'Tis the same fantasy of the mind
So let's close our eyes and travel
To the alchemy of your beauty
That morphs my soul
So let's kiss and unite
With the magic in your eyes
The planets' polar reflection
Your fairy floating finger

Charms my heart
With one touch
With one spell of your passion

Tears like rain can be of happiness or pain
I cry thy beauty in a thousand wishful words

To forge my nights magical
To impel my days miracles
My life is wonder in the light of your love
All I need is one glance
To dream about you forever

I am a scholar of your love learnèd at the first touch of your lips

This love exists
It's the passion I create
The Zulu say
Magic takes time
Well I have all my life
To bewitch you of my beauty
Of my charming eyes
Of my enchanting voice
Of my fascinating stature
Of my enamoured locks
Of my spellbound bosom

I am a scholar of your love learnèd at the first touch of your lips

Fear not
I bare the Scorpio's sting
Overcome this venom in faith
And you are truly living life
Avoid this venom in fear
You are surely death

Listen 'Tis the Sound of Poetry

I used to feel your nervousness
But I blocked it with my faith
Time is your face
Every ticking second is your blink
Kissing you is kissing time
Were they glorious?
Were they victorious?
Those who conquered love
And called themselves brave
I am still here defeated by your beauty
Believing in Amor Vincit Omnia
I am victorious I am glorious
Because I still love you

I patiently wait here
Young and restless
Just to hear your voice again
This music I hear
Steals my breath away
Every verse I hear
I think of you
I think of your love
Your kiss is my breath of life
I bow to thee my love

We walked in the dark
It seemed like the only place you could shed a tear
In the shadows of the night
Crying about how you were going to miss me
I never felt so special
I never felt a force as strong as your love

The first poem I ever wrote
Was seeing you
Seeing your nose and its birthmark
The captivator of sensational beauty

The first planets I ever saw
Were your two eyes
Looking at their circumference
A deep constellation of color and radiance

The first tropical fruits I ever tasted
Were your luscious lips
Licking a luring nectar
For me to fall on hungry and helpless to kiss

I Closed My Eyes and Believed

The first thing we manifested
Was the combination of our planetary eyes
I sensed my sight I saw you and you were real

The second thing we manifested
Was the sound of our voice a musical conversation
I sensed my hearing I heard you and you were real

The third thing we manifested
Was everything the unification of our divine hearts
I sensed my heart I felt love and this love is real

The fourth thing we manifest
Is aroma your flowery scent my musky redolence
I smell your hair I smell your skin and you are real

The fifth thing we manifest
Is our taste for each other the miracle of a kiss
I sense your lips I taste their movement and you are real

The sixth and last sense we manifest
Is our embrace the softness of our hands caressing
I sense your touch I feel you but are you real?

I Choose You

I choose not to watch a film in hopes that
I can identify my love for you with a character
Instead I choose to watch the sky and follow
The unfolding scenery of the clouds and identify your
Face in a form of beauty that the sun ever so reflects
I choose not to sleep in hopes that I may
Lucidly have you next to me
Instead I stand in the night to stare at the moon
With a stupor and concentration for a constellation
Of a slumbered sky's scenery
Amidst this hypnotic horoscope
I discovered a new zodiac
Your face
And your two twinkling eyes

I choose not to breathe in hopes that I may be
Vital to survive vivacious to live and virtuous for life
Instead I choose to breathe in belief that air is love
And love is life even so your kiss is my only capsule of air
Your love is the very beat of my heart
And your beauty is the omnipotence
Of this wonderful world

By the tides of the Moon
The waters of the earth
All the red roses that bloom
And the blood of my worth
May you know that my love for you is like energy and God
Both can neither be created nor destroyed
In simple words I choose not to say any more other than
I ♥ you to ∞

Love like Lotus

Ahh
Open your heart to mine like the petals of a lotus to the sun
Water this love with your words
I will water this love with my actions
Let us awaken to balance
Yin and Yang
Awaken to love
Close your eyes
Believe in my touch
I am real
Let us cocreate our destiny
Begin with this kiss
A sound to echo through the valleys of paradise
Continue uttering the sound of divinity
I will worship your ecstasy
Peace is our essence
Understanding is our virtue
There is no explanation but to keep soaring
We are moving through the realm of waves
Thoughts and unity and oneness with nature
We are realizing through the world of forms
Watch these particles mould to reality
Don't utter a question my love
Let us manifest
Let us water it all with our tears
Gratitude and grace
Om

Love of the Zodiac

I am the earth she is the water

We merge perfectly and caress so tenderly

I feed her with love and she feeds me with passion

My love is her passion her passion is my love

I am hard and she is soft

This splendid space is called unity

It is what sages render as Yin and Yang

Where heaven and earth live in harmony

Where different poles attract naturally

This is how we bind

So perfectly

Magnetic Love

No matter what I do
To run away from you
You are reincarnated
In everything I experience
Music is about your love
Birds sing of your voice
The sun shines your smile
In the clouds I see your face
At night I see your eyes
In the stars in the skies
The moon glows your spirit
Distance is just a word
Your thoughts affect my psyche
I close my eyes and you are here
Kissing me holding me breathing my air
Nature is perfect so is love
Let us not add to it
Our shallow understandings
Which turn into misunderstandings
Love is natural
Let us just add to it
Our hearts

Baffled Zodiac

Our time zones have confused our zodiacs
You are tomorrow
I am today
This distance will reap great things
Every day we are apart
Bit by bit we build this bridge
So that one day confusion is lost
Misunderstanding is lost
And all that is found
Is love

Contiguous Countenance

We acknowledge our distance
From each other
And choose to glance
At figments of surrealism
But with love all is possible
And when our distance is bridged
And we are close enough
To breathe on each other
We will not be able
To acknowledge reality
Or time
Because I love you
Acknowledge this kiss
Let's fly

Tangled?

Love gets complicated
When you look too far into the future
Love only exists
For this moment
When I stare into your eyes
Reflecting the starry night a pupil of the moon

Love gets complicated
When you use too much intellect with the relationship
Love always exists
For every moment
When we both walk in faith
And both hold hands in trust

Love gets simpler
When we only intervene with prayer
Love is always here
Forever for you and me
Belief is all you need
Close your eyes to first see

Guide Me O Divine Spirit

On this carpet ride
O'er the 7 seas
Under the moonlight
And starry sky
Safely set me by the window
Of my dearly beloved
That I may see her dream
That I may see her breathe
While I passionately and patiently
Wonder and Wish
Seeing the reflection of my tears
And the reflection of the moon
And the reflection of a shooting star
The window is foggy
I have drawn a heart with my forefinger
There is a strong gale
My beloved hath awoken
And hath softly walked to the window
She hath stood beholden by my heart
And a drop of tear
The window is foggy
She hath drawn a heart with her forefinger
There is a strong presence
My love hath awakened
Find me amid the clouds

What If

If I told you I love you in my language
Would you cry?
Maybe I'll see a tear drop in your eye
If I told you that
I have never told anyone
In my language in my country in my birthplace
Other than you
Being the first to hear *Nakupenda*

Why Wait for Love

It took a minute

For you to say I love you back

Why should your love wait?

You ask me

Will the butterflies always be here?

I say

As long as the sun shines on our love

Forgiveness

I still forgive you
For calling this fantasy
We are floating
But your eyes are closed
You are dreaming in reality
Daydreaming in the night
You are having visions
Inexplicable
Don't complain
To understand is not to understand
Let go of this ego
I have nothing to prove
But this mountain to move
To have a clearer path to paradise
Love is real
Not an illusion
Believe in my touch
Let us conjure a kiss
Trust with your eyes wide shut
Believe with your heart wide open

My Only Need

All I need is your love
And your stare
To know that you're there
Forever
Forever by my side
And in my heart

All I need is your Kiss
And your touch
To know that you're in me
Together
Together with me
And I in you

Possibility

Anything is possible
But there are some things
That are impossible
Like for me to love another
Other than you
The thought itself
Is inconceivable
Me speaking of it
Is utterly blasphemous

Only

Pleasure is only now
Romance is only today
Passion is only tonight
Desire is only months
Longing is only every moment
Love is only forever
Love is only truth
Truth is only love
Love is only you and me
Love is only love
Love is only love
You are all I only have
You are the only one I love
The only one I truly love
The only true love
The only
One
&
Only
Love

My Only Request

All I ask for is your embrace
Your embrace to know
That you are real
I want to feel your composure
Melt into mine
In one moment in time
To seal this deal of love
We are meant to be
Now my poetry speaks its reality
Now my dreams awaken congenially
I can't stop staring into your opalescent eyes

Rose Bush

You're still there peeping at me through a rose bush
All I see is those bezel gem like hazel eyes

I could live in this moment
Forever
One memory to remind me
Of nature's beauty and bounty

I am a dream undyingly searching
For a portal to awaken into reality and awareness

You consume me with your presence
Your eyes drain my soul out
To spill of desire for your touch
How are we so ever connected?
My memory sings the song of the stars
We are meant to be
We are meant to be

What is life without singing?
What is love without longing?

I wrote about love and I found you

What is True Love?

True love is not a bare dazzling diamond
It is a hidden diamond in the rock

Obsession is glistening gold
It is but pyrite

True hope is an opal
It is inside the heart of a tourmaline

I am real love a silent emerald
But will you choose to wear me?
Will I choose to wear you?

Life together would be the process

Polishing starts today

Love is already there
The journey begins here

If love were to be seen
If love were to be seen

The heart would be the most precious jewel
To wear and to gleam

I Suddenly Awoke and Wrote of You

If love were truth and if truth were love

Just knowing you I know for certain both I have

If love is true and if truth is love

Then you have always been my true love

Our Love

The mystery behind your words

Sometimes it's fun

Sometimes not

Your love for me is unchanged

Unconditional

I know you always come back

That is why this is true

I have spilled my heart for you

As the ocean spills on the earth

I have conquered fear in faith

Faith in me is so strong

It is unchanged and unconditional

Like your love

My love for you changes

Even though I don't like changes

When I accept changes

I know it is only for the best

And the best is now arrived

We are the best of lovers

People stare and wonder

Mesmerized by your fluid motions

Hypnotized by my sturdy notions

You and I

You are the moon
I am the waves
The gravity of your love
Invokes and provokes
A tossing and a turning
Of
A tumultuous and turbulent
Sea
That runs of wine
Sweetest of nectars
Through my veins
My heart beats with pleasure
Upon your taste
To just think of you
Is euphoric
No conjured magic
Nor opiate
Could reach this feeling
Is there a remedy for love?
Is it a wonderful sickness?
Is there a cure for cupid's arrow?
Is it a joyful curse?
Why do we tarry?
Let us sail the sky

Tears at Midnight

Tears reflecting the beautiful moonlight
A full bright moon on my birthday
Bright and round through the trees
And branches and shadows of leaves
A lonesome moon glowing white
A clear night's sky
Starry scenery
Tears of joy and wishes of truth
Tears of happiness desires of love
Tears of bliss nothing but peace
The moon shifted and the shadows lifted
Behold there is love
For there is a heart of love I see
Shaped in a halo 'round the moon
N' through a tree

Thief

Your beauty stole my sleep

Your lips of liquor lured me

Into drunken emotions

The aroma of your perfume

Is incense that burns

Ecstasy in my body

Your voice kidnaps my manhood

Your words are my poetry

Break this spell you have cast upon me

My thoughts cannot breathe a second of rest

Without thinking of you

Why are you the only one amongst all the ones?

Am I bewitched by blind love?

Or love that is first to my sight?

Does destiny draw us down here together?

On this earth?

My love you make me magic

Loss or Gain?

Will I lose something to get something?

Why compare this with love?

If I lose the world I gain eternity

If I lose your love I gain eternity of loneliness

We are all connected

Lose not

There is nothing to lose

The world is my love

Come and gain everything in me

But first you must step over the ocean

And lose fear and nervousness and anxieties

You are not alone

When you feel my hand in darkness

There is light to guide us to the sun

You are now with me

Let us make a home in the sky

And plant a seed of hope

Don't worry

We can free these butterflies in our bellies

Once in a while

When we lay to unite

Floating in the night

Bathing in the moonlight

We'll never be lost

Love is our home

And this is what I feel

Awareness is Connection

Come sit on my lap

Perch a nest in my heart

I am connected to you

You are connected to me

Let us open our awareness to love

Let it never lack

Let us plant a seed of hope

To grow into a tree of trust

To grow roots of belief

And any doubts and fears

Would just be wind

To shake us and awaken us

To trust deeper

To love deeper

Let us burry our egos

And harvest peace

Let us drink of gratitude

And feast of grace

Worries are excuses

Of too much comfort

Let us fly with risk

Because we are growing

Out of this world

We are born to be divine

Time is creation

Our destiny is a manifestation

Crimson Love

Love is so special
It can neither be taught nor learnt
It is a seed we are born with
One that grows
In the pretty garden of the heart
As it ripens through life
Some bad things may occur
Thus making sharp edges
Some never to be forgotten
Like scars scourged into stories so deep
Or so outwardly protruding
But beauty is nevertheless
Like unto a rose whose petals so dear
One sacrifices pain for one embrace
And for one glance at beauty in blind love
Such that truth is a rubicund reflection
Dear drops of sanguine tears
To merge with the crimson rose
Of love

My Miracle is your Love

If I go mute
The one thing I will struggle to communicate is
I love you

If I go blind
The only thing on my mind is
Your eyes and their beauty

If I go deaf
The one thing I will always hear is
Your voice and its music

If I am any of these
I know I will still taste your kiss
I know I will still smell your skin

Your love is my miracle
To speak forever of my love for you

Your beauty is my masterpiece
For me to paint your portrait in the canvas of nature

Your voice is my song
For me to dance in jubilee like angels of heaven
One of which you are

My Meaning of Life and Death

The throb of my heart
Your soft breath on my ear
The heightened thoughts of my mind
The core of your eyes
A reflection of the stars
Your featherweight lips
As thin as clouds
Disbelief of my existence
This feels beyond goodness
This moment jetting my spirit
Through time and space
The past the future
My life with no love
This was before
My life with you
A future of divinity
Infinity of love and desire
You have metamorphosed my being
The last beat of my heart
Your soft tears warm
Trickling down my wrinkled face
Last kiss of your lurid lips
I have departed
To be united with the infinite consciousness
My meaning of life
Love
My meaning of death
Life
And its endless meaning of love

My Last My All

If the world were to end
I pray that I see you once on your birthday

I pray that you will look into my eyes and hear
My heart cry out *I love you*

If there is one question I would like answered
Before I die *what is love?*

And my last breath would be *I love you*
My last thought would be *your beauty*

My last blink would be *your eyes*
Eternity for me is *your love*

-The End-

www.ingramcontent.com/pod-product-compliance
Lightning Source LLC
Chambersburg PA
CBHW032100230426
43662CB00035B/885